FAR

FROM THE

OUTSIDE

FAR FROM THE OUTSIDE

A Collection of Poetry
and Spoken Word

PJ

PHOENIX JAMES

FAR FROM THE OUTSIDE

Copyright © 2022 Prince-James Harrison.

For any questions about usage, please email contact@PhoenixJamesOfficial.com

First Edition: 2022

ISBN: 978-1-7396788-0-7 (Paperback)
ISBN: 978-1-7396788-1-4 (Ebook)

Cover Artwork & Design by Phoenix James.
Book Design & Formatting by Phoenix James.

Visit the author's website at www.PhoenixJamesOfficial.com or email him at phoenix@PhoenixJamesOfficial.com

DEDICATION

To those who relish words of positivity
To those who seek gems of inspiration
To those who quest, knowing deep inside
There's so much more to life out there
For each of us to be, see, do and become
To your peace, freedom and happiness
And to those still searching on the outside
For that which can only be found within
I hope this helps you along your way

And to a young boy
Who always knew
Long ago

Thank you for sticking around
And never letting me stray
Too far from the inside

May this ignite a fire in your restless soul
And bring a warming joy to your heart.

CONTENTS

ALL THINGS

All things
Are possible
And nothing
Is beyond reach.

AMAZING THINGS

As each day passes
My beliefs
Are being even further reinforced
That when we choose
To believe in ourselves
Wholeheartedly
Not only do we excel
As well as radiate positive energy
And inspire others
To aspire to greater heights too
But we also at the same time
Set in motion
A series of internal
And external vibrations
Through our thoughts
Our attitudes
And our actions
Which the universe absorbs
And responds to
In accordance to our wants
Needs and desires
Opening a gateway
For amazing things to happen
And take place in our lives
Very thankful.

ANYTHING

Your limitations exist
Only in the mind
You can do anything
You can be anything
Many will say you can't
Know that you can
Capture your dreams
Exceed your potential
Be all you can be.

ASCENSION

That's a great question
What direction
Do I feel
My soul is drifting in
Or going in
What is my soul's direction
That's pretty intense
But to answer it
I feel like my soul
Is in a good place right now
I feel like there's a release
Like a lifting
A shifting of things
I feel like I've been releasing
A lot of things
Which is giving my soul a lightness
That's allowing it to ascend
In a positive way
I feel like
I've been holding onto
A lot of things for a while
And I feel like this year
Things have been happening
That have allowed me to

4

Let go of a lot of things
And allowed that freedom feeling
That weight to be lifted off
Peace and fulfilment I feel
Is what's been happening
In terms of that
Just in a good place generally
It's been release
I've been able to free myself
From a lot of things
Sharing a lot of myself
And that's been allowing me
To shed things
And release things
That are allowing me to feel lighter
And in that feeling lighter
My soul is feeling lighter
My soul is feeling uplifted
And rising
And energised
Peace
If I was to say
What direction it's going towards
I would say peace
Going to a place of peace
And fulfilment

There's a lightness to it
That kind of airy feel
When you feel
You've let go of some things
That were holding you down
Like if someone's attached a balloon to you
And you rise a little bit
And someone attaches some more balloons
And then you rise a little bit more
And the more balloons that they attach
You start lifting up and going higher
My sunset is definitely coming up
This is the beginning of it
I'm feeling like this is the beginning
Of that that sunset
You can feel yourself
Coming out of the shade
Have you ever watched the ground
And you see the sun moving
And then the shade is disappearing
And the sunlight is coming in
Closing in on the shaded area
That's how I feel
That's happening with my soul right now
Ascension
I feel that contentment

And that fulfilment
Coming from everything
That's been going on with me
In the past year
A major shift is what I'd call it
Sharing content has really helped me
To do that
Letting go of things
That I was just holding in my head
And maybe not even aware of
That were there
But only when I start talking
They come out
That's been freeing
What direction is my soul going in
Wow
That's a first
Apart from when
You go past a church
And there's someone outside
Screaming at you with a pamphlet
Apart from that
It's a pretty deep question
On this subject of soul shifting
I feel like I'm revisiting an old self
I think it's part of this shift

I think it's part of this soul shift
As I like to call it
Because I'm meeting people
From my past
And they're being presented
Every so often
There is a new person from my past
Just appearing
It's almost like a test
And also like a lesson at the same time
And it's very eye-opening
To recognise that these people
Are just showing up one by one
I'm trying to watch it from outside of myself
So I don't get caught up in it
But I understand what it means
And what it's there for
So I can take the lesson from it
Because I know it's for a reason
I just have to keep myself out of
Getting caught up in this thing of old times
And stay from outside of it and observe
What that lesson is
From each of those individuals
What they've come to teach me
They are people

8

That I had connections with
But never actually met in a proper way
When I say connections
They are people that I knew of
It felt like those connections
Never completed themselves
Unfinished business
Like someone had come
To give you a message
But they never got to fully give it to you
So they've come back
To give you the full message
It's like that
And now I need to pay attention
To what it is we missed
The first time around
That's how it feels
Eyes open
Chakras grounded
There's definitely
A lot of lessons being learnt
And definitely a lot of
Soul shifting going on right now
Clarity is one of my
Favourite words at the moment
There's a lot of clarity now.

BE

I've wanted to quit
And give up
Many times
I've just
Never had the time.

BELIEVE

Do not let anyone
Ever
Make you feel
You don't have
What it takes
To achieve your dreams
Not ever
Believe
You can achieve
Those
And more.

CATALYST FOR HAPPINESS

I'm thinking I feel okay
I feel a lot better
Than I did a few years ago
Traveling
Exposure to different scenery
Different people
Different environments
Just a chance for the mind to roam
In a different way
When you're in different places
You're not used to
Your mind expands
That's made me feel
In a lot better place
Than I did a few years ago
Not just travelling to the country
But when you're there
Travelling around
And meeting people
Having different experiences
That definitely was the catalyst
For new happiness
I feel good
I started this saying I feel okay

But I feel a lot better than okay
I do
I think turning forty as well
There was a shift
You realise that you're forty
And you're lucky if you get another forty
The clock's ticking
So that all happening at once
I think made me look at my life
And where I am
And if I was happy or not
And then realising
That I wasn't as happy as I could be
And making the changes
That's what's brought me to that place
And I can only do that in solitude
Which traveling allowed me to do
Because I was travelling on my own
For the most part
I feel more at peace
Even if I'm not at total peace
I am a lot closer, a lot closer
There's a couple more things
I want to wrap up
And then I'll be good

I want to bring family closer
I think families are important
I feel events have happened
Out of my control
That now that I've found
My own happiness
And my own peace
Or closer to that ultimate peace
I feel I'm in a better place
To have effect
Realising my power more
I realise that I have
Enough power to change things
Sometimes you don't realise that
When you're not in that place
That's going to happen
That's already happening
Based on the fact
That I've arrived
At a new place within myself
It's almost like a by-product
Or a natural progression of that
Even that's beautiful
It's already in motion
It's never perfect
Nothing's ever perfect

But getting closer to that perfection
Is a beautiful feeling
We make plans and God laughs I hear
An important thing of all of this
Is that everything that's happened
Has allowed me
To find more of myself
And be at peace showing myself
That's a massive part of it
Finding yourself
And then being happy to show that
And then feeling comfortable enough
At a place where you're ready
To let people see that
Is nice
That's what I think people refer to
When they say that you look happy
You look at peace
Whatever they're getting
Whatever is coming off of me
That they are seeing
That is it
I'm happy as fuck right now
Truth be told
You know
There's a lot worse things going on

And I like to document
As much of it as I can
As I go along
You know
The journeys
The happiness
I want to look back
And remember these moments.

CHOICE IS OURS

I'm a strong believer
That we make our own luck
And that we can
Turn things around for ourselves
At any moment
So I think
If something bad is happening
I can choose how I feel about that thing
I can choose to think
Oh nothing ever goes right for me
This hasn't worked out
Just like the last thing
I'm cursed
It's always negative
I'm supposed to be a failure
I have the choice
Of how I determine that thing
Or how I look at that thing
I can also then say
Oh this is another test
This is going to make me stronger
This is preparing me for something
This is good
I can grow from this

This is going to strengthen me
I can choose how I look at it
I think the choice
Is always ours
How we view a thing
And then obviously
Based on how we look at that thing
And how we choose to view it
That will affect how we act
And then that
Will obviously affect the outcome
So it can go either way
For me
I was exposed to that way of thinking
As a teenager
Fortunately
I had the right input around me
To change my thinking
Or affect my thinking
To lean on a more positive side
When negative things happen to me
Or things that could be
Considered negative happen
Or when I experience something
That isn't the most favourable
Of things to happen

I had a process in place
Due to the things I had around me
And the right voices around me
And the right influences around me
That made me think in the way
That would produce a positive outcome
Or a positive thought
Or a positive action
Rather than a negative one
A negative thought
Oh why is this happening to me
Oh it's the end of the world
Instead of what it should be
Which is
This is something
That's going to strengthen me
There's something I could learn from this
I can grow from this
What does this mean
This is another opportunity to go again
And do it even better
When I was seventeen
Just going on to eighteen
I was exposed to NLP
Which stands for
Neurolinguistic programming

I was doing someone's hair
At his house
I was barbering at that time
And he had a cassette tape playing
On his little stereo
A man speaking
Sharing an empowering message
And I was drawn in by the information
That was coming out of the speakers
It resonated with me
We spoke about it a while
And then I asked him
If he would lend me
A couple of the tapes
Which he did
And I listened to that stuff religiously
I just liked what was coming out of it
I loved the positivity
I loved the whole thing
About how we can manage our mind
And manage our thoughts
Affect the outcomes that we get
And the results we produce
And as a teenager you're impressionable
I was influenced by it
And it shaped my outlook

On negativity
And positivity
And how we process information
All of that
What we think is negative
And what we think is positive
And can we affect that
Are we at the mercy of it
Or can we control it
And affect change
And all of that
And I grew up from there
With that mindset
And it's only just got stronger
The more I've stayed around
That type of information
And what happened with listening
To people like the man on the tape
I got to learn about more people
Who spoke in the same way
And taught the same stuff
Then I started reading books
I learned about other people
And other cassette tapes
And books
And reading that information

It just got more and more and more
And strengthened that thing
That was strengthened as a teenager
It just got more and more and more
And I just got immersed in it
And I further immersed myself in it
Because it was just a new thing
It made sense
And then it began to affect my writing
And some of the things I was saying
In my poetry
And some the stuff I was performing
It began seeping into my material
The way I wrote was affected by it
Because obviously
When the mind is affected
What you're producing creatively
Is affected
So it just became
More and more a part of me
When I would speak
People would want to hear that stuff
More and more
Because it resonated with them
And it just became a thing
And I've been that way ever since

So when a negative happens
Automatically
My mind goes to a positive
More than a negative
What's the solution
Over what is the problem
Rather than
Oh my God
Look what's happened
This is the end of the world
Or
What does this mean
What can I learn from this
How can I grow from this
You see the difference?
And that's what the exposure
To NLP
At an early age
Did for me.

FOCUS

Consistent focus
Dedication
And hard work
Pays off
Constant procrastination
And laziness
Will cost you dearly.

FOCUS ON THE POSITIVES

Do you know
What I would do
If I was doing
Some kind of exercise with you
This is something
I did with my friend
Who's being let go
From her job
And it's the whole thing of
She's a little stressed out by it
And the whole finding a new job
And where is she going to be now
In life kind of thing
So what I got her to do
Was to make a list
Of all the things
That would be good
About leaving
And starting new
What's good about this happening
I got her to make a list
Of those things
And she said
Doing that really helped her

To get some focus
And some clarity
And some kind of direction
On what's next
Now that this has happened
And she can't change it
That's the kind of exercise
I would do with you as well
In your situation
Where you're at
To look at what is good about it
What is actually good
About being there
And in terms of
You saying about doing a vlog
If you had a camera right now
I'd get you to talk about that
About what you would do
And about being different
And documenting
I would get you to talk about that
If I was mentoring you
Or teaching you
Or guiding you in that way
That's what I would get you to do
I would get you to make a list

Of all the things that are good
About where you are now
And what is positive about it
And talk about that on camera
So then it's kind of like
Killing birds isn't it
You're going to be creating content
And you're also going to be
Turning a negative
Potentially negative
Into a positive
That's just a thought I just had now
As we were talking about it
That's what I would do
I would get you to
Look at the positive stuff
About where you are right now
And at the same time
In the process
Create content
To just talk about that
What is good about it
You'd feel better
And you'd have some content to share
You might have to
Dig a little deep

To find it
But it's there
There's always a positive
There's a positive to every situation
That's it
If you're willing to be
Open-minded and look
And dig
When it seems like
Everything is negative
There's always some kind of
Positive angle on everything
It's just the balance of life
It's just the way it is
It's yin and yang
There's always
A positive to be found
Always.

FOR ALL WHO PERSEVERE

Our continuous
And unwavering persistence
Dedication
Perseverance
And hard work
Will eventually pay off
We will soon receive
The full
And proper recognition
Appreciation
Honour
And respect we deserve
Those who judge us
Count only our shortcomings
Laugh at us
And oppose our success
Shall only be laughed at
Judged
And encounter the opposite
Of our success
All of our digging in the dark
Alone
Throughout many late nights
And early mornings

Towards our goals
And dreams
Shall be brought to light
None of our efforts
Or sacrifices
Are or shall be in vain
In abundance and appropriately
All we have done
And all we do now
Will be fully recognised
And rewarded
We shall never give in
Give out
Or give up
It's all about progression
We shall continue
Moving forward

For my friends
Who persevere.

GO FOR IT

Be it
Do it
I say
I'm one of those people
That believes
That you can do anything
You put your mind to
That's pretty much it
Everything else
Once you put your mind
To becoming a certain thing
Everything else
That you require
To achieve that goal
Will come to you
That's just how
The universe works
Just go for it
Once you decide
That's what you want to do
Things will start
Opening up to you
That will get you there
That's one of the things

I firmly believe
So my advice
Just go for it
Do it
Be it.

GREATEST LEVERAGE

In terms of succeeding
In anything we're trying
To succeed in
Any place we're trying to get to
In terms of dealing with the world
I think one of the things
We need to definitely highlight
Is our differences
Those are the things
That make us
Those unique things about us
Those are the things
That are our greatest parts
The greatest leverage for us
The things that make us different
That we didn't like as a kid
Because we were singled out for it
Because of that thing
That thing
Is the thing
That often makes the person
The thing.

HIGHLY RECOMMENDED

Over the past few days
I've somehow
At very different times
And in very different situations
Been fortunate to meet
And be in the company
Of some really cool characters
And we've together
Found laughter
And made huge
And hilarious jokes
Out of some of the smallest
And silliest things
I wish I could run through
Each of the scenarios with you
Or draw you pictures
Or better still
Put you right into those moments
For you to experience them too
I have truly laughed so much
Until my sides hurt
And I can't breathe
Even now
I can still feel my sides a little

And flashbacks
Of some of those discussions
And exchanges
Are still making me chuckle now
I laugh often
But I seriously
Haven't laughed this much
In a while
I'm sure you can recall a time
When you laughed just like that
Laughter is truly
A great feel-good medicine
For all things
Many say it's the best
It's also very infectious
I definitely recommend it highly
If you feel you have nothing
To laugh about
Just laugh at yourself
And share the joke
It's great to laugh.

HONOUR THYSELF

Get to know
Who and what
Is not for you
Not just because
Other people say so
But because you know
In your heart
That these people
That this person
That this thing
Is not for you
Get to know who
And what
Is not for you
And move on
Not every person
And not every thing
Is for you
Get to read the signs
Get to understand
And do the right thing
For you
Sometimes
You just need
To separate yourself

We're only here
For a brief time
There's nothing wrong
In taking yourself away
From situations
And people
Things that don't serve you well
That don't serve your spirit well
There is no wrong in it
It's justifiable
There is no good
In spending your time
Around people and things
And experiences
That are not going to elevate you
In the direction
You want to go in your life
Staying in uncomfortable situations
There's absolutely no need
There is nothing dishonourable
In going your own way
Away from people
Things and situations
That do not serve your spirit well
Please take note
And do what's right for you.

IF NOTHING ELSE

We are neither less
Nor more
Than the sum total
Of all we believe
So a person thinks
So a person is
The mind controls the body
And thoughts control actions
With our thoughts
We create our world
Little by little makes a lot
The little world laughs
While the big world
Cheers us on
As we set out
To achieve our goals
And dreams
Progression begins with progress
Success comes in many faces
And makes many friends
But is faithful to none
And comes not without
Some suffering and sacrifice
Preparation

Perseverance
Practice
Patience
Pressure
And persistence
Are powerful
And make perfect
Nothing is just by chance
Each person you meet
Will either add to
Or take away from you
Everything that happens
Happens for a reason
Whether we are late
Or whether we are early
The universe
Is ever present
And always on time.

IMAGINE

It is quite possible
That some day
In the future
A group of people
Are going stumble across
A person
Who is doing
Exactly what you've done
And are doing now
And will each tell the world
How amazing
And unique
That person is
And what a genius they are
And that there has never
Ever
Been anybody
Quite like them
Imagine.

IN THE GAME

In the game of life
We can sit on the sidelines
All day long
Calling ourselves competitors
And point fingers
At the field
And criticise
The actual players on it
About what their doing
And how their doing it
And what they should be doing
Or not doing
Or could do better
As a lot of people choose to do
It's safe
It's easy
And in many cases
A great way of diverting criticism
From ourselves
Making us feel better
About our own shortcomings
However
I personally
Find it far more fun

Challenging
Exciting
Rewarding
And empowering
Being in the game
Playing the game
Enduring the trials
Highs and lows of the game
Whilst learning the game
Growing from the game
Meanwhile staying in the game
With my eyes on the game
It's really hard to score
When you're not even
In the direction
Of your field
Much less your goal
Eyes on the ball
And keep it moving.

INSPIRATION

It's not from where
You get your inspiration
That's important
It's where you take
Your inspiration to.

IT'S TIME

You are greater
And far more powerful
Than you realise
Your possibilities
To become
Whatever you desire
In your life
Are endless
And infinite
Your capacity
For the achievement
Of any level
Of success
You can imagine
Is beyond anything
You've ever thought of
It's time
To become
All you can
And are meant to be.

KNOW WHEN IT'S TIME

It's all about positivity
You just have to know
When it's necessary
To separate yourself
From certain things
And certain people
Because you just know
No good
Is going to come of it
So you've just
Got to know
When that time is
And be perceptive
Tune into your
Perceptive energy
And just know
When it's time
To separate yourself
From certain people
And certain things
No going back.

LETTING GO

The thing with me is
I'm trying to talk a lot more
About the things I don't talk about
Or haven't spoken about before
Because
I'm feeling that freeing feeling
From doing so
That release
And I'm enjoying that freedom
And the feeling that comes from that
I'm at a stage now
Where I'm releasing it to the world
I don't really care who knows
It's not private anymore
It's not secret
It's not like
Oh I can only tell my best friend
It's like I get something now
Out of sharing those things
That we keep
We keep to ourselves for so long
Because of fear of whatever
Whatever those fears are
Whatever makes us

Keep those things to ourselves
I get more out of sharing it now
That's my therapy
Sharing it
Releasing it
It's out now
There's nothing to hide
And hold onto
It's freeing
It's really freeing
It's like trying to fly
With weights attached to you
It's like trying to fly with sandbags
Attached to you
And then you drop them off
One by one like an air balloon
You drop them off
And you start to lift up
That's what it feels like
When you start
Letting go of certain things
You start to feel that light feeling
That weightless kind of feeling
You feel a bit lifted
Each time you let go of something
That you've been holding for so long

It's like someone
Who's got a deep dark secret
And they've been keeping it
And then they let it go
They can't hold it anymore
And they feel that weight
Off of their shoulders
No matter how bad it is
The secret they've been carrying
For so long
They let it go
And then they can exhale again
What it is might be really bad
But they're free
They feel free now
Because they don't have to drag
That secret around anymore
That weight on their back
That's what this year
Has been like for me a lot
Letting go of a lot of those things
Letting go of those sandbags
That weigh us down
People don't see me
As a talkative person
Because I don't talk

48

Unless I'm on stage
Delivering something
Or speaking
Or performing poetry
Or in a movie
Delivering some lines
People aren't going to see me speak
I don't speak
This is the first time
People are hearing my voice
And that's exactly what I'm talking about
I haven't even started saying anything yet
This is just like exercising the muscles
You know
Getting ready
Like how you stretch
Before you do the actual thing
This isn't the actual thing
I'm just stretching
This is just feeling it out
Feeling out the ground
Just a little test run
This isn't the singing
This is just vocal training
I haven't said anything yet
I've got so much stuff to let go of

And to release
And to speak about
To express over time
And there's no rush
I have the patience
There's absolutely no rush
Everything will come out in its time
At the right time
Because I'm not afraid anymore
The door is open now
So anything can come out now
The door is wide open
When the door is closed
Nothing can come out
You know
Unless
The door gets opened for a second
And shut again
Something might seep out
But now the door is wide open
So anything can come out
At any time
Why now
I can't answer
Because I don't know
The answer to why now

50

But I do know it's now
And I know it's time
And that's why it's happening now
Because it's time
But outside of that
I don't know why now
It's just time
Nothing before it's time
Like Jesus of the Bible
They say
That he didn't say anything
For the benefit of mankind
Until he was thirty-three years old
So imagine
All of what he had within
That he had to give
It took thirty-three years
Before he went out
And spread the gospel
Imagine
Nothing before it's time
I look at it like that
You said
Is this how I write my poetry
Well
This is the poetry

This is it
This is it as it's going to be
It's being formed as I speak
It's about everything
That it takes
To make life a poem
It's about all the elements
All come together as one
All the elements that it takes
To form that thing
It's all part of it.

LIVE YOUR DREAMS

Take action
Explore new avenues
Release your fears
Exercise your full potential
Be all you can be
Live your dreams.

MAGIC MANTRA

All things are possible
And nothing is beyond reach
Little by little makes a lot
It's all about progression
Never give up
All good things
Come to those who work
It's not who you know
It's who you know who
Actually gives a shit
Keep going
And keep it moving.

MISSION STATEMENT

I just quickly want to remind you
If you haven't already
Done so or set out plans to do
To remember
To make some time
To sit down
In a quiet space
And write out
Your mission statement
Yes, your mission statement
Don't wait
Until the new year
Has already begun
Though it's never too late
To write down our plans
And intentions
Many of us
Make the bad choice
Of putting it off
Or not doing it at all
And find ourselves
In the dilemma
Of feeling behind
And chasing the year

Instead of being more prepared
And focused from the start
Setting off with our ideas
Without proper planning
Is very much like
Quickly reading a map at home
Putting it down
Then setting off on the journey
And trying to remember
Or guess what we saw on the map
And which direction we should go
It wastes valuable time
That could be used
Far more efficiently
And effectively
Towards our aims
And desired outcomes
It's great to have all of our goals
Grand schemes
And dreams
And new year's resolutions
Inside of our heads
And be able to talk about them
In depth
And know them back to front
But once we have carefully

Taken time to write them down
Clearly and precisely on paper
They become
Something even greater
They become
A sort of binding contract
With ourselves
Committing us
To what we say we want to achieve
Subconsciously
And on a deeper
And far more concrete
And meaningful level
A clear map
Towards our intended destination
That we are far more likely to reach
When on the road to success
It's just like being in a car
We have to be mindful
Not to get distracted
Sidetracked
Or lost
In this regard
It's also easy to crash and burn
A mission statement
Is a sure way

To make sure
We stay alert
And focused along the journey
Be safe
Mission statements
Are very powerful
And they work
I'm currently fine tuning mine
As you read this
And getting it ready for the road
Let's be purpose driven
With our purpose written.

MOUNTAINS

Staring at the distant mountain
Frustrated it was so far from reach
Continued walking towards it
And there I was
Staring down from its peak.

PEOPLE, THOUGHTS & THINGS

Surround yourself
With people
Thoughts
And things
That continuously
Uplift
Motivate
Drive
And inspire you
Remind you
That you are greater
And stronger
Than your situation
Or circumstance
Show you
That there is magic
And a lesson
In every moment
Encourage you
To believe
That you can always
Do
Learn
Grow
Achieve
And become more.

PHILOSOPHY OF POSITIVE

That is all I'm about now
Just being around
The right people
Positivity is high up
On the list
It helps so much
It really helps
For me
It's all the
Subconscious stuff
That you take in
When you're not
Thinking about it
There's always a negative
And positive thing going on
It's just balance
It's either going one way
Or the other
It's never really in the middle
It's either you're around
Mostly negative
Or mostly positive
And if you're around negative
All the time

You might not even
Be thinking about it
But it's going in
The subconscious mind
Is always working
It's always absorbing
Not even things
That you necessarily say or do
But things that you're just
Listening to
The people you're around
And the things that they're saying
And the way that they behave
You may not even be aware of it
That you've got negative friends
You may not even be aware
That all your friends are negative
They're just your friends
But you're absorbing
All of that negative energy
All of the time
And then wondering why
Things aren't right
And those people
That always
Have an answer for everything

It would be good
If the answer was positive
That's fine
If they've got an answer for everything
But it would be nice
If the answers were positive
If every answer was positive
Because that means
All you're absorbing
From those people is positivity
That would be great
But unfortunately
It's not always that way
I think a lot of people
Are just wired to be defensive
Like a goalkeeper
Everything that's thrown at them
They have a way of
Knocking it down
Or knocking it out
Or knocking it away
Everything that comes at them
They always have a way
Of knocking it away
Or grabbing hold of it
And dissecting it

And then discarding it
It's never
Yes, this is positive
I'm going to take this in
It's always a deflective thing
There's always
Picking holes in things
There's always a thing of
Never absorbing
Yes, this is positive
This is great
This is good
Yes yes yes
It's never that
It's always the opposite
Resistance to positivity
It's so important
To be around positivity
There's a saying that I hear a lot
People want you to do well
But never better than them
So what does that
Actually mean then
So people are okay to hear
That you're doing your thing
And you're doing whatever

And you're progressing
And they'll big you up
To that degree
But once you're progressing
Ahead of them
Or it seems that way
Or appears that way
I think it then changes
That's what that saying is implying
It changes
It shifts from boosting you up
To tearing you down
You just need
To be around positive energy
Twenty-four seven
That's just real
It's all about positivity
I'm just not interested otherwise
The only time I want to see negativity
Is when I'm ready
To just have some target practice
When I'm really high energy
And I just want to
Knock some negativity down.

POSITIVE ADDICTION

I feel a lot of people
With an addictive personality
Not limited to
But especially with
My star sign
Virgo
They are the people
That you tend to find
Get into drug addiction
Alcohol addiction
Because they've got
An addictive personality
So you have to be careful
What you get into
Overeating is another one
Gambling that's another one
Overindulging
So I have to really watch myself
And I like
That I've found
Something that's cool
I can over indulge in it
And it's progressive
It's productive

I'm recording parts of my life in bits
It's not dangerous
It's not going to kill me
At least not in a drug
Alcohol
Overeating
Gambling way
It's pretty cool
I miss when I don't do it
When I don't create I notice it
It's like I need my fix
I need to write
I need to film
I need to record
I need to document
I need to get my thoughts
And ideas
And my presence
Out to the world
And preserved
It's definitely a thing
I get itchy
I need that hit
I need that fix
It's so my thing
Thankfully

It's not food
It's not all the vices
All the negative vices
That are not good for you
Sex
How dare I forget
Sex is another one
That people get addicted to
And that doesn't always end well
So I'm not doing too bad
With my addictive personality
Needs right now
Weaknesses you could even say
I've fallen into one that's
Not too harmful.

POSITIVE INFLUENCES

I was just blessed
To fall into the influences
Of things like
Personal development
And motivational speakers
And NLP
And stuff like it
People with provocative ideas
About the way we think
And how we use our brains
Listening to their work
Listening to their words
What they're talking about
And taking that in
I was fortunate
To have it as a young person
As a teenager
And that had an impact on me
And that kind of helped me
Stay on the right path
I guess
In a way
From a road that
I could have gone down.

POSITIVE OVER NEGATIVE

Talk about the anxiety
When you're out of it I think
If you do it from a place
Where you're down
It might not come out positive
Be aware of it
And then do it from
An analysis point afterwards
Which I think may be
The way you may
Deal with the anxiety thing
Talking about it
From outside of it
Not actually feeling anxious
At that time
And I think that's the best place
Because then
People can relate to the fact
Oh you've been there too
Oh you've been to the cinema
By yourself
Rather than
I'm at the cinema by myself
I feel so shit

It's a bit different I think
It could be not so positive
To just present the negative
But more so
How you came out of it
And how you deal with it
Whatever it might be
That's the thing
That's the positive side of it
The positive over negative.

POSITIVE SIDE OF EVERYTHING

I get down days
Pretty much like anyone else
But I think
What has happened is
I've kind of learnt
To handle those down days
In a particular way
That doesn't make me spend
Too long
Within those down days
Or dwelling
On negativity
My coping mechanism
Is always
Realising
That it's not the end
Of the world
It's not a death situation
I'm not dying from this
Whatever this thing is
At the moment
It's about being able
To take myself
Out of the moment

And look at how small it is
Thankfully I haven't had
Anything in my life yet
That has made me feel otherwise
But there's always a time
Within that frame
Of that thing happening
Whatever it might be
That I could step outside
And look at it
Look at the bigger picture
As they say
And realise
That it will pass
And it's just a moment
And also
The fact that I can grow from it
I can learn from it
It's something to expand me
To make me stronger
Like looking at the positive sides
Of everything that happens
And how I can use it
As something to empower me
To the point where
I'm able to do it

Quicker and quicker
I dwell for less time
In those situations
Because it has become
A mechanism
That just happens automatically
And I'm able to get out
Of that negative place
Much quicker
So it may seem like
I'm always happy
And I'm always on
Because I'm not spending long
In that place
I'm a human being
So things will affect me
Just as much as the next person
But how long I stay in that place
Or how I choose to look
At the situation may differ
Which means
I don't spend too long there
Some people will say
Why did this happened to me
This is the worst thing
That could have possibly happened

This is the end of the world
And other people will say
Well this is changed
This is going to make me grow
This is going to make me
Have to look at myself
And be more
And that's going to make me
A better person
I'm going to learn from this
I can share it with others
It's going to expand me
It's not going to crush me
Rather than looking it like
The whole world is on top of me
Instead
What will it mean
When I climb out from this
And get on top of it
What will it make of me
This is the making of me
This thing that has happened
This is an opportunity
To prove
That I'm a champion
And I can overcome.

POSITIVITY ALWAYS WINS

I'm all about the positive
100% positive
My positive shield
Is so strong
And forceful
That negativity
Just bounces off
It's like Captain America's shield
Or Thor's hammer
It's just got some power
Against certain things
That's how it should be
There's another way
But I don't like that way
There's an alternative
To positivity
But I never
See it work out for people much
I don't see it doing
Anything beneficial
So I avoid it
I avoid the negativity
It's all positivity all the way
I have not known

Any negative thinker
To have a successful positive life
Until they start living
And thinking in positive ways
So I choose positive every time
The most negative situation
That I'm faced with
Or that I experience
I always look for the positive
In the situation
If there's an ounce
Of positive in there
A little glimpse of positive
I suck it out
I take it
I extract it from the negative
And turn it into a positive
Like turning a sock inside out
You reach inside
And you grab the toe part
From the inside
And you pull it through
The other end
Or like a glove
That's exactly what I do
With negativity

Turn it inside out
I have to pull out
Any positive bit of it
Right through
That's a crazy analogy
I don't know where that came from
But it works in my mind
The most negative situation
If I can't find a glint of positive
To draw from it
I make it up
I create something positive
About the situation
That I can learn or gain from
Or share with others
Always always always
Looking for the positive
In everything
Always always always always
It's just the way I'm wired
I just don't know any other way
I'm just programmed that way
I made myself into a new man
By taking in new information
And motivational teachings
And new thought practices

78

I started listening more
At age seventeen
I was exposed to NLP
When you're a teenager
You're impressionable
I got into that
And I was just continuously
Soaking up recorded material
I had cassette tapes
And I wanted more tapes
Then I went and bought books
As a teenager
That's the type of stuff I was absorbing
Neurolinguistic programming
Was going into my young teenage brain
So that's just one example
Of the type of wiring I have
I think ninety-five percent solution
Five percent problem
Rather than the other way around
That's in everything
I don't really know
How to think negative
In a situation for long
If I ever do
I think it's just down to influences

I just think it's what you're around
What you're exposed to
What's in your ear
What kind of people you mix with
Even the music you listen to
The books you read
The films you watch
The places you go
It all has an impact
Your parents
And what they put into you
It all has an impact
Majorly
Don't start me off
On positivity
You've got prosecution
And the defence
My defence is strong
I'll win my case every time
You put your negative opposition
Against my positivity
I will beat you
And I will not stop
Until you're beaten down
Until you submit
The two forces together

In a room
And my side being positivity
There's no match
Because I've just
Wired myself that way
Because it's the only way.

PUTTING IN THE WORK

I'm looking at
The next five years
Not next month
I'm looking at the fact
That if I continue doing
What I'm doing now
Everything
That I could possibly want
Will come to me
I won't have to go looking for it
That's just how it works
It's doing the work
And that's
What I'm focused on right now
I can't just
Put up a few videos
And think
How many subscribers can I get
How much can I get paid
It's just not the way I think
It's going to work out for me
I get it
This whole plane runs on money
People want to make money

People want to do things
And enjoy life
I get that
But it's not where
My income comes from
I'm not depending on it
To get rich
Doing the work counts most
Everything else
Comes after that
Ask me in five years
My eyes are closed right now
My eyes are not even open
My eyes are closed to all of that
Because I just want to do the work
I know if I look up in five years
I'll be probably blown away
By what's happening
Consistency and patience
Is the game
That's the whole game
Now that I've learnt patience
What do I do now but apply it
And then let it all play out
All these people that we talk about
They put work in

Before they were anything
I've just stepped in
I'm a baby
I want to do the work
I want to close my eyes for five years
And put in some seriously hard work
I know that all the things
That people want now
When they've just been
Doing it for five minutes
I will get that
By putting in
A hundred times more work
Because
You're not going to get it
For no work
When they haven't even
Left the gate yet
I get it
People just
Don't want to do the work
They take one look at the work
And they think that's daunting
Who wants to invest time
Into doing something
For five years

Just close their eyes
And get on with it
Who wants to do that
People want to do something
For three months
And expect
To see rewards straightaway
Five years is nothing
It was long to us
When we were kids
Five years was forever
But now we've grown up
In our thirties, forties whatever
We see that five years
Is the click of your fingers
That's why I'm happy
I'm happy to put my head down
And just create and produce more
And not look
For any rewards immediately
I know they will come
And here I mention five years
But could be ten, fifteen or more
I'm a firm believer in
If you build it
They will come.

SEE DIAMONDS

As one door closes
Another one opens
Rarely are truer words spoken
The universe
Works in accordance
To our most passionate desires
Deepest fears
And strongest inner convictions
Thoughts become things
Guide yourself
In the direction of progress
A diamond in the rough
Becomes a diamond on the cuff
Pressure is preparation
Stay faithful
Stay focused
Keep busy
Keep working
Never give up
Never give in
And never stop shining
Better will come.

STAND GUARD

Definitely don't overthink it
It does take practice
It's destructive to overthink it
It can be destroying
To allow those negative things
To affect you
To allow people's negative opinions
And negative ideas
To influence you
Your thoughts
About you
Can be most detrimental of all
I think over time
It's easier
Dealing with
Building yourself up
In a way
That doesn't allow it
To penetrate you
In the way
That makes you think
Negatively about yourself
Or your work
Or what you're pursuing in life

And I think that
Over the long term
That is an easier thing
To build up that resistance
Against negativity
I think that's easier
Than dealing with the effects
Of being soul destroyed
By people's opinions of you
Realising that you allowed
Outside forces
To affect you
And your opinions
About your dreams
And what you already know
And to change your mind
I think over the long term
That's more destructive
Looking back and thinking
That it wasn't even true
It's just what I allowed
People to influence
In my mind
You're just basing it
On someone's opinion
Who doesn't even necessarily

Have any expertise
Or any real education
In the subject
Or thing you're doing
They just have an opinion about it
Which is not valid in anything
Not grounded
In any real substance of anything
It's just an opinion
That someone's just
Put out there
And it's affected you
Or you've allowed it to
And then looking back
When the time has passed
I think that can be
More destroying to you
Than just dismissing it
As just an opinion
That stands on nothing
As a teenager
I grew up listening to
People talking about
Standing guard
At the door of your mind
How important it is

To protect yourself
Because there's going to be
The naysayers
There's going to be negative people
There will be those
Who talk you down
And tell you
You can't do it
That's it's not good enough
And this standing guard
At the door of your mind
It's protecting you against that
A lot of people
Leave their door open
And unguarded
And they allow
These people's opinions
To get in there
And affect the way
They think about themselves
I think it's a good thing
To keep in mind
That you have to stand guard
At the door of your mind
You have to be there
To guard yourself

From those things
Those things that can get in there
And play with you your thoughts
About yourself
And what you do
And what you're capable of
It is about the conversation
You have with yourself
And that must always
Be positive one hundred percent
Not allowing anything external
To influence it
If it's not beneficial
To the way you're thinking
Always thinking positively
Not allowing anything in
That is negative
That is going to counteract that
That's what the standing guard is for
Protecting that internal voice
And making sure
Your internal voice
Is always positive
In the direction
That you want to go
It's about positive internal dialogue

Working on that
Keeping it positive
One hundred percent
Keeping your mind exposed
To positive information
To positive energy
To positive voices and sounds
And influences
And shutting out
Everything that opposes those
Being in control
Of that dialogue
Of what you let in
It's not easy to do
It's very hard
It's difficult
It takes practice
But what's more difficult
Is dealing with
Wow
Look what's happened
I've let all this negativity
These outside external forces
And elements
And voices affect me
And it stopped me

From doing what I knew was right
What I wanted to do
And I could have succeeded in
If I had just shut that door
And kept them out
And told myself
What I already know
That I can do this
I'm capable
And I can achieve this
That I'm good enough as I am
That's harder to deal with
Because then
You're looking back in regret
It takes time
And it's not easy
But I know what's harder
I know which I prefer
It's light work
When you think of it that way
Just don't take it on board
Let's focus
On that internal dialogue
That allows you
To do what you want to do
In the most positive way

Stand guard at the door of your mind
If it's not positive
Don't let it in
You're not coming in
If your name is not positive
You're not coming in
Over time it gets stronger
And stronger and stronger
And easier to do
Until the point
Where it becomes automatic
You see it from a distance
Only let in the positive stuff.

SWIM OR SINK

I had a conversation yesterday
And I was saying
It's because
They come to this country
And they have to make it work
They come with nothing
And they've given up
What they had at home
To come here for a better life
And they've come with nothing
So they have no choice
And they've come with family
And small children as well
So they literally
Have to make this happen
They've got no other choice
But to make it happen
There's no other family here
To depend on
No other handouts
So they have to swim
There's no sink
They have to swim
People who come
From other countries

And succeed in other places
Or in this country
Where we're comfortable
We're here already
We're in it
We've got things to fall back on
We can go and claim benefits
We're not immigrants
We could just
You know
Go to our mothers
Or fathers
Or some other family member
Or wherever
We can get by
There's always
Some kind of help available
But they
Have to jump in
No support group
No outside help
No handout
It's swim
We've got to swim
Or we're going to just drown
And that's it
We're not drowning
We're going to swim.

THE JOURNEY & THE PROCESS

About the waiting thing
To really make anything of anything
You have to love the process
That's with anything
You have to love the journey
More than the actual getting there
Because you're going to spend
Most of your time
In the process of getting there
As opposed to getting there
Getting there is the thing
You finally get there
And that's it
Then it's what next can I do
But until you get there
It's all journey
It's all that trudging uphill
Until you get to the peak
Of what it is you're trying to get to
To the pinnacle
To the mountaintop
So you have to love the journey
More than you love getting there
That's what it is for me

I don't love the journey of acting so much
I love playing roles
And I love performing in that way
And pretending
And I love
The whole pretending thing
Of acting
Like when we were kids
We pretended to be things
And it was fun
And you could be creative with it
And I love that
I just don't love the whole machine of it
As an adult
And the whole process of
Going through it
You have to love that
I love the processes of other things
And I'm more passionate about those
I love the process of writing
I love the process of
Putting a piece together
And the process of learning a poem
And performing in front of an audience
And everything in between
Whether it's recording it

Performing it
Writing it
Editing it
Adding a word here
The sound of it
I like the rhyme
I love the whole process
From scratch
From a blank page
To the stage
I love the whole process
And you have to love anything
That you want to enjoy being a part of
That you're willing to put that time
And energy into
You have to love
And I don't love the process
Of acting
In that way
The creative side of it yes
But not the whole machinery
Of what you'd have to be a part of
To get to that place
If you wanted to be Mr. Hollywood
Oscar-winning
You know

Blockbuster movie
There's a whole process
You'd have to go through
Auditions is one of them
And I absolutely don't like auditions
I don't like the process of auditions
And being a waiter
Waiting around
Waiting for my agent to call
Waiting to hear if I got the part
Waiting when I get on set
Waiting for my makeup
My costume
All of this stuff
Waiting to see if I'm even in the film
When it comes out
Waiting for the film to come out
The whole process
It's all waiting
You're a waiter
And full respect to anyone
That is in that arena
And I have a lot of actor friends
And it's for them
Because they love the process
They love that process

Auditions are like nothing to them
Auditions stress me out
That's the honest truth
You have to be self-aware
And I don't feel it
In the way that they feel it
I'm coming from
A different place with it all
I'm coming from a place of
Having the control
Of putting out my material
How I want to put it out
Not waiting for anyone
To tell me it's good
Not waiting for anyone
To tell me
Yes we accept you
Yes we want you
I'm coming from a place
Of spending so long
Having the control
And doing what I want to do
And taking my stuff
Direct to the audience
I write a piece
I learn it

I perform it
It goes straight to the audience
I record something
It goes straight to the audience
It's been like that
From way back
Since 1998
So to now come into a world
Where you have to have
Somebody else tell you
If you're good enough
I really struggle with
That's one of the reasons I hate auditions
Because in terms of
What I was doing before
I don't have to wait on anyone
Even now
Putting out content
I don't have to have anyone tell me
If my content is good or not
I just share it
And let the world decide as a whole
I'm used to that
And that's why I love this place
I am at right now
I've come full circle in a way

A lot of people
That knew me before acting
Didn't like it
When I started acting
I think they didn't like that aspect
Of me giving up that control
I think they saw it as
Me giving up my power somewhat
But it took me a long time
To see what they were seeing
Why they didn't like it so much
I thought they were just haters
I think they saw me stepping down
From something that was great
That I had all the control over
I think they saw that as me
Stepping away from my gifts
To hand myself over to somebody else
To judge and to be the jury
It took me a long time to learn that
Thankfully I learnt it
In the end
But it took a while
I guess I needed to go through that
To see what they were seeing
I always thought they were just hating

But it wasn't that at all
It was love more than anything else
I wouldn't take away from it
I wouldn't say
If I could go back I wouldn't do it
Because it's helped me so much
In what I actually do now
It's actually added more
More strings to my bow
It's added more to me
I have more to give now
Through all of that experience
I have so much more to give
Than I had ten years ago
Legacy
I like that word a lot.

THE ULTIMATE GOAL

Don't forget
Every moment is something
And there's an audience
For every show
I think it's always
The right time
Reason being
Every moment is something
And there's an audience
For every show
Two things I've learned this year
We're all just making it up
As we go along
No one really knows do they
You look at your grandparents
And you realise
That they didn't even know
Or know even now
Everyone is just trying to figure it out
I think we spend our whole lives
Trying to figure out the meaning
Of why we're here
The purpose of life
The direction we're going

I think there's just more days
Where we feel comfortable
With the direction we're going in
Than other days
Some days we feel like
Oh yeah
This is it
This is what it's all about
And other days we're like
What hell was that
Everyone is still guessing
You find a level of happiness
And then you're cool with that
But you're not sure
That's the way
You should have gone
But you're happy
With the way it has turned out
The choices you made
That's a win if you're happy
But we're still guessing
It's never a negative
It's a positive
Happiness is the ultimate goal
But ultimately
We're still guessing

We're still hoping
We are making the right decisions
Along the way
No-one comes
Having it all figured out
We're all working towards
And that's what life is about
The journey is what it's most about
The experiences
The learning
The ups
The downs
It's all part of it
It's all a part of the final piece
It's exciting
It's exciting not knowing
Exciting times
I'm super excited
About what's to come.

TO A YOUNGER ME

What advice
Would I give myself
If I was given the opportunity
To go back in time
And meet myself
What would be
My most important advice
To my younger self
If I was able to do that...

Be patient
Just be patient
You're on the right track
You're going the right way
You're doing the right thing
All you need to do
Is maintain patience
Just be patient
That would be the advice
I would give my younger self
If I could go back in time
And meet him
Why I would say that
To my younger self

Instead of other things
That could be considered
Such as mistakes
Or making wrong decisions
They all stemmed
From impatience
In my experience
Every one of them
All stemmed from impatience
Looking back now
Being the older self
When I look back
At my younger self
And all the actions I took
And the decisions I made
They all stem from one thing
And it was impatience
That's why
I would give him
That advice
That one thing
I think would be
All he would need
To be patient.

WELCOME CHANGE

I'm sure a lot of the things
I said ten years ago
I wouldn't say now
Or the ways I thought
I wouldn't think now
Or those ways of thinking
Have changed
And thank god
That's life
We're supposed to change
Things are supposed to change
We're supposed to change our opinions
Everything is change
Nothing stands still
That's the only thing
That you can bet on
Is change
That's the only thing that's guaranteed
Above everything else in this life
Is things are going to change
We should evolve
We should change our minds
We should outgrow
And think differently

Can't stand still
It's impossible
I should be able to come back
In ten years
And say
Oh I don't actually
Think that way anymore
Yeah I said that then
But my opinions have changed on that.

WINGS

Don't forget
You have wings
They could do with some use.

WITNESS PROTECTION

I've been a witness
To seeing
The following in action
So many times
And what I witnessed yesterday
Was no exception to the rules
I am compelled to testify
Being nice to others
Doesn't cost a thing
And is often
Highly rewarding
However
Not being nice
Can cost you dearly
Immunity is the key
Karma will never
Spend a single day locked away
Therefore
We all get caught eventually
My written statement above
Is the closest
I'll probably get to you
Regarding sentencing
So do pay close attention

To these words
Down the line
If you are guilty
Simply hand yourself over
To the law
Get with the program.

WORKS OF WISDOM

It's never a failure or a cop out
To go back to a nine-to-five
If it helps to meet the end goal
A vehicle heading to a destination
Often needs to reroute
Or be reconsidered
Or often be changed completely
For another mode of transport
Needs must
If returning to a nine-to-five
Is necessary to help the journey along
Then so be it
It's just a way to assist one
To get to where one is heading
It's simply a reviewing of one's map
Along the way
And adjusting
To what best takes one onward
To reach the end point
The necessary means of travel
And sometimes
The abandoning of that means
For another
To reach the intended destination
Is never to be considered a cop out
Or a failure.

ABOUT THE AUTHOR

Phoenix James is an award winning Writer, Poet, Author and Spoken Word Recording Artist. He began performing his poetic words live on stages across the UK in 1998. His debut spoken word poetry album, *The A.R.T.I.S.T,* was released in 2000. His first limited edition printed collection of poetry, *To Whom It May Concern,* was published in 2003. He has toured and performed his poetry internationally since 2004. He has appeared in films, on television and radio shows, and collaborated with other artists, singer-songwriters, actors, musicians, filmmakers and producers. In 2013, he wrote, directed and produced the feature length mock documentary film, *Love Freely but Pay for Sex.* Phoenix James has written, recorded and released several spoken word poetry albums including, *Phenzwaan Now & Forever* (2009), *A Patchwork Remedy for A Broken Melody* (2020), *FREE* (2021), *Haven for the Tormented* (2021), *With All That Said* (2022), and *Remixes* Volumes: 1 & 2 (2022).

If you enjoyed reading this book, please leave a review online. The author reads every review and they help new readers discover his work.

PHOENIX JAMES

Photo by Phoenix James

Phoenix James lives in London, England.

Connect with Phoenix James on his online social media platforms via www.linktr.ee/ Phoenix_James and say you've read this book. To contact or learn more about Phoenix James and his creative journey or to receive updates via his Newsletter Mailing List, visit his official website at www.PhoenixJamesOfficial.com

Phoenix James Official